90 Days
of
Encouragement

Inspiration to Uplift Your Spirit
and Feed Your Soul

Darryn Zewalk

WESTBOW
P R E S S®
A DIVISION OF THOMAS NELSON
& ZONDERVAN

WestBow Press books may be ordered through booksellers or by contacting:

WestBow Press
A Division of Thomas Nelson & Zondervan
1663 Liberty Drive
Bloomington, IN 47403
www.westbowpress.com
1 (866) 928-1240

ISBN: 978-1-5127-5569-5 (sc)
ISBN: 978-1-5127-5570-1 (e)

Library of Congress Control Number: 2016914590

Print information available on the last page.

WestBow Press rev. date: 09/14/2016

Day 1

Remember if God isn't for it, then ignore it.

James 4:7 - Submit yourselves therefore to God. Resist the devil, and he will flee from you.

Day 2

I love Jesus above all.

Matthew 6:33 - But seek ye first the kingdom of God, and his righteousness; and all these things shall be added unto you.

Day 3

What God says, He does.

Jeremiah 29:11 - For I know the thoughts that I think toward you, saith the LORD, thoughts of peace, and not of evil, to give you an expected end.

Day 4

God must be #1.

Proverbs 3:6 - In all thy ways acknowledge him, and he shall direct thy paths.

Day 5

Jesus is always available, all you have to do is call Him.

Romans 10:13 - For whosoever shall call upon the name of the LORD shall be saved.

Day 6

There's nothing like God's love.

Romans 5:8 - But God commendeth his love toward us, in that, while we were yet sinners, Christ died for us.

Day 7

Don't worry about your situation, remember, whatever is, God is much greater and will give you strength to overcome it.

1 John 3:20 - For if our heart condemn us, God is greater than our heart, and knoweth all things.

⊙❀❁❀⊙

Day 8

I am trusting in God.

Proverbs 3:5 - Trust in the LORD with all thine heart; and lean not unto thine own understanding.

Day 9

You're favored by God.

Psalm 5:12 - For thou, LORD, wilt bless the righteous; with favour wilt thou compass him as with a shield

Day 10

Keep your eyes on God.

Psalm 16:8 - Keep me as the apple of the eye,
hide me under the shadow of thy wings,

Day 11

God is the reason I live.

Acts 17:28 - For in him we live, and move, and have our being; as certain also of your own poets have said, For we are also his offspring

Day 12

Whatever you do, don't unfollow God.
Hebrews 10:26 - For if we sin wilfully after that
we have received the knowledge of the truth,
there remaineth no more sacrifice for sins.

Day 13

I've got confidence in God.

2 Corinthians 3:4 - And such trust have we through Christ to Godward

Day 14

LORD please make me aware of things that are not of you, so that I can separate myself.

2 Corinthians 6:17 - Wherefore come out from among them, and be ye separate, saith the LORD, and touch not the unclean thing; and I will receive you,

Day 15

God is still in control.

Psalm 22:28 - For the kingdom is the LORD's: and he is the governor among the nations.

⁘᯾᯽᯿⁘

Day 16

The LORD is my strength at all times.

Psalm 28:7 - The LORD is my strength and my shield; my heart trusted in him, and I am helped: therefore my heart greatly rejoiceth; and with my song will I praise him.

Day 17

All you need is God.

Philippians: 4:19 - But my God shall supply all your needs according to his riches in glory by Christ Jesus.

Day 18

Just as I am God accepted me.

John 3:16 - For God so loved the world, that he gave his only begotten Son, that whosoever believeth in him should not perish, but have everlasting life.

Day 19

**When God is in the midst, everything
in your life will be fixed.**

Zephaniah 3:17 - The LORD thy God in the midst of thee
is mighty; he will save, he will rejoice over thee with joy;
he will rest in his love, he will joy over thee with singing.

Day 20

If God is not in it, there's no way you can win it.

Proverbs 21:30 - There is no wisdom nor understanding nor counsel against the LORD.

Day 21

Jesus you are everything to me.

Psalm 84:11 - For the LORD God is a sun and shield: the LORD will give grace and glory: no good thing will he withhold from them that walk uprightly.

Day 22

I asked the LORD to change me; He rearranged me. Remember, He's never failed and never will.

Psalm 136:1 - O give thanks unto the LORD; for he is good: for his mercy endureth for ever.

Day 23

God is too good to not be praised.

Psalm 145:9 - The LORD is gracious, and full of compassion; slow to anger, and of great mercy.

Day 24

The best deal is to stay in God's will.
Romans 12:2 - And be not conformed to this world: but be ye transformed by the renewing of your mind, that ye may prove what is that good, and acceptable, and perfect, will of God.

Day 25

Trust God against all odds.

Nahum 1:7 - The LORD is good, a stronghold in the day of trouble; and he knoweth them that trust in him.

Day 26

God loves us all.

Proverbs 8:17 - I love them that love me; and those that seek me early shall find me.

Day 27

There's no day without the blessings from God.
Psalms 118:24 - This is the day which the LORD
hath made; we will rejoice and be glad in it.

Day 28

The grace of God can carry you through anything.

Philippians 2:3 - Let nothing be done through strife or vainglory; but in lowliness of mind let each esteem other better than themselves.

Day 29

God will help you just call on Him.

Psalms 50:15 - And call upon me in the day of trouble: I will deliver thee, and thou shalt glorify me.

Day 30

Joy is coming, just hold on and trust in God.
Romans 15:13 - Now the God of hope fill you with all joy and peace in believing, that ye may abound in hope, through the power of the Holy Ghost.

Day 31

No greater love than Jesus giving His life for us.
John 15:13 - Greater love hath no man than this,
that a man lay down his life for his friends.

Day 32

**Just the thought of spending eternity
with God is worth praising Him.**
John 17:3 - And this is life eternal, that they
might know thee the only true God, and
Jesus Christ, whom thou hast sent.

Day 33

God reigns Forever!

Psalm 146:10 - The LORD shall reign for ever, even thy God, O Zion, unto all generations. Praise ye the LORD.

Day 34

**The best is yet to come. Believe in
God and trust His process.**

1 Corinthians 2:9 - But as it is written, Eye hath
not seen, nor ear heard, neither have entered
into the heart of man, the things which God
hath prepared for them that love him.

Day 35

The love of God is more than you'll ever need.
2 Corinthians 9:8 - And God is able to make all grace abound toward you; that ye, always having all sufficiency in all things, may abound to every good work:

Day 36

When you are going through a struggle hold on to God because there's a blessing on the end of it.
1 Corinthians 10:13 - There hath no temptation taken you but such as is common to man: but God is faithful, who will not suffer you to be tempted above that ye are able; but will with the temptation also make a way to escape, that ye may be able to bear it.

Day 37

There is no battle God cannot win.

Jeremiah 20:11 - But the LORD is with me as a mighty terrible one: therefore my persecutors shall stumble, and they shall not prevail: they shall be greatly ashamed; for they shall not prosper: their everlasting confusion shall never be forgotten.

Day 38

When God is on your side...that's all you need.

Romans 8:31 - What shall we then say to these things? If God be for us, who can be against us?

Day 39

Through disappointment, still trust God.
Psalm 34:18 - The LORD is nigh unto them that are of a broken heart; and saveth such as be of a contrite spirit.

Day 40

I can't make it without Jesus.

John 15:5 - I am the vine, ye are the branches: He that abideth in me, and I in him, the same bringeth forth much fruit: for without me ye can do nothing.

Day 41

When God says, "Stop it," you must drop it.
John 8:47 - He that is of God heareth God's words: ye therefore hear them not, because ye are not of God.

Day 42

God is magnificent!

Psalm 145:3 - Great is the LORD, and greatly to be praised; and his greatness is unsearchable.

Day 43

Don't worry about your haters. Put all your focus on your creator.
James 4:7 - Submit yourselves therefore to God.
Resist the devil, and he will flee from you.

Day 44

God's grace is sufficient.

2 Corinthians 12:9 - And he said unto me, My grace is sufficient for thee: for my strength is made perfect in weakness. Most gladly therefore will I rather glory in my infirmities, that the power of Christ may rest upon me.

Day 45

God's always got your back.

Deuteronomy 31:6 - Be strong and of a good
courage, fear not, nor be afraid of them: for the
LORD thy God, he it is that doth go with thee;
he will not fail thee, nor forsake thee.

Day 46

God never forgets you.

Isaiah 49:15 - Can a woman forget her sucking child, that she should not have compassion on the son of her womb? yea, they may forget, yet will I not forget thee.

Day 47

God will give back everything the devil stole.
Job: 42:10 - And the LORD turned the captivity of
Job, when he prayed for his friends: also the LORD
gave Job twice as much as he had before.

Day 48

God will level every devil.

Romans 16:20 - And the God of peace shall bruise Satan under your feet shortly. The grace of our LORD Jesus Christ be with you.

Day 49

Faith = Trusting in God and His timing.
James 1:3 - Knowing this, that the trying of your
faith worketh patience.

Day 50

Jesus lifted.

Psalm 40:2 - He brought me up also out of an horrible pit, out of the miry clay, and set my feet upon a rock, and established my goings

❧❧❧

Day 51

Make God first in your purpose.

Proverbs: 3:6 - In all thy ways acknowledge him, and he shall direct thy paths.

Day 52

When God is involved problems get solved.
Philippians 4:6 - Be careful for nothing; but in everything by prayer and supplication with thanksgiving let your requests be made known unto God.

Day 53

Be a Christian with a mission.

Mark 16:15 - And he said unto them, Go ye into all the world, and preach the gospel to every creature.

Day 54

Let God be praised every day.
Psalm 113:2 - Blessed be the name of the LORD
from this time forth and forevermore.

Day 55

No matter what, I will put my trust in Jesus. He works for my good.

Jeremiah 17:7 - Blessed is the man that trusteth in the LORD, and whose hope the LORD is.

Day 56

Just the thought of God in my life is all I need.
Psalm 16:5 - The LORD is the portion of mine
inheritance and of my cup: thou maintainest my lot.

Day 57

The LORD is forever thinking of you.
Psalm 115:12 - The LORD hath been mindful
of us: he will bless us; he will bless the house
of Israel; he will bless the house of Aaron.

Day 58

When God says no...Let it go.

Proverbs 28:9 - He that turneth away his ear from hearing the law, even his prayer shall be abomination.

Day 59

God is awesome!

Psalm 47:2 - For the LORD Most High is awesome, the great King over all the earth.

Day 60

God is always with you.

Ezekiel 36:25 - Then will I sprinkle clean water upon
you, and ye shall be clean: from all your filthiness,
and from all your idols, will I cleanse you.

Day 61

I surrender my life to you LORD.
1 Corinthians 10:31 - Whether therefore ye eat, or drink, or whatsoever ye do, do all to the glory of God.

***

Day 62

God is amazing.

Romans 8:35 - Who shall separate us from the love of Christ? shall tribulation, or distress, or persecution, or famine, or nakedness, or peril, or sword?

Day 63

God = The greatest love.

Proverbs 8:17 - I love them that love me; and those that seek me early shall find me.

Day 64

God is always awesome.

Psalm 68:35 - O God, thou art awesome out of thy holy places: the God of Israel is he that giveth strength and power unto his people. Blessed be God

Day 65

I tried to live my life without God, it wasn't worth it.

Romans 8:28 - And we know that all things work together for good to them that love God, to them who are the called according to his purpose.

Day 66

Never doubt God.

Matthew 21:21 - Jesus answered and said unto them, Verily I say unto you, If ye have faith, and doubt not, ye shall not only do this which is done to the fig tree, but also if ye shall say unto this mountain, Be thou removed, and be thou cast into the sea; it shall be done.

Day 67

You can't...God can.

Matthew 19:26 - But Jesus beheld them, and said unto them, With men this is impossible; but with God all things are possible.

Day 68

All praises go to God.

2 Corinthians 1:3 - Blessed be God, even the Father of our LORD Jesus Christ, the Father of mercies, and the God of all comfort;

Day 69

There's never a test without a test. So, embrace your test knowing that God will use it for a bigger purpose.

James 1:12 - Blessed is the man that endureth temptation: for when he is tried, he shall receive the crown of life, which the LORD hath promised to them that love him.

Day 70

When God tells you no, don't question Him...
Just let it go.

John 14:15 – If ye love me, keep my commandments.

Day 71

The love of God conquers all things.
1 Peter 4:8 - And above all things have
fervent charity among yourselves: for charity
shall cover the multitude of sins.

Day 72

God will always love you.

Romans 8:37 - Nay, in all these things we are more than conquerors through him that loved us.

Day 73

Rest in knowing you are favored by God.

Psalm 5:12 - For thou, LORD, wilt bless the righteous;
with favour wilt thou compass him as with a shield

Day 74

Forgiveness = Healing

Ephesians 4:32 - And be ye kind one to another, tenderhearted, forgiving one another, even as God for Christ's sake hath forgiven you.

Day 75

Real strength is you relying on Jesus.

Psalm 27:14 - Wait on the LORD: be of good courage, and he shall strengthen thine heart: wait, I say, on the LORD.

―――❦❦❦―――

Day 76

Don't lose hope, always keep your trust and faith in God.

2 Samuel: 22:31 - As for God, his way is perfect; the word of the LORD is tried: he is a buckler to all them that trust in him

Day 77

**There's no way I can make it
in this life without God.**

1 Corinthians 10:13 - There hath no temptation
taken you but such as is common to man: but God
is faithful, who will not suffer you to be tempted
above that ye are able; but will with the temptation
also make a way to escape, that ye may be able to
bear it.

Day 78

God is undefeated.

Joshua 23:14 - And, behold, this day I am going
the way of all the earth: and ye know in all your
hearts and in all your souls, that not one thing hath
failed of all the good things which the LORD your
God spake concerning you; all are come to pass
unto you, and not one thing hath failed thereof.

Day 79

Thank you LORD for all you've done & what you're about to do.

1 Thessalonians 5:18 - In every thing give thanks: for this is the will of God in Christ Jesus concerning you.

❧❦❧

Day 80

There will never be another love that will ever compare to the love God has for you.
Romans 8:39 - Nor height, nor depth, nor any other creature, shall be able to separate us from the love of God, which is in Christ Jesus our LORD.

Day 81

Praise God Forever.

Psalm 145:2 - Every day will I bless thee; and I will praise thy name forever and ever.

Day 82

You are God's creation.

Ephesians 2:10 - For we are his workmanship, created in Christ Jesus unto good works, which God hath before ordained that we should walk in them

Day 83

When God is your motivator, He will silence your haters.

Psalm 143:12 - And of thy mercy cut off mine enemies, and destroy all them that afflict my soul: for I am thy servant.

Day 84

Never ignore the Power of the LORD.

Colossians 1:16 - For by him were all things created, that are in heaven, and that are in earth, visible and invisible, whether they be thrones, or dominions, or principalities, or powers: all things were created by him, and for him:

Day 85

**God is my strength today, tomorrow, &
forevermore.**

Ephesians 6:10 - Finally, my brethren, be strong
in the LORD, and in the power of his might.

❦

Day 86

God will never leave you alone.

Hebrews 13:5 - Let your conversation be without covetousness; and be content with such things as ye have: for he hath said, I will never leave thee, nor forsake thee.

Day 87

TGIF = Thy God is Flawless.

Psalm 18:30 - As for God, his way is perfect:
the word of the LORD is tried: he is a
buckler to all those that trust in him

Day 88

I will trust in God.

Isaiah 12:2 - And it shall come to pass in the last days, that the mountain of the LORD'ₛ house shall be established in the top of the mountains, and shall be exalted above the hills; and all nations shall flow unto it.

Day 89

God is everything.

Colossians 1:17 - And he is before all things, and by him all things consist.

Day 90

Trust God always.

2 Samuel 22:33 - God is my strength and
power: and he maketh my way perfect